# Away She Goes

## Riding into Women's History

by Wim Coleman and Pat Perrin
illustrated by Valentina Belloni

RED
CHAIR
•PRESS•

Please visit our website at **www.redchairpress.com** for more high-quality products for young readers.

 EDUCATORS: Find FREE lesson plans and a Readers' Theater script for this book at www.redchairpress.com/free-activities.

## About the Authors

**Wim Coleman** and **Pat Perrin** are a husband and wife who write together. Their more-than-100 publications include plays, stories, articles, essays, books, classroom materials, and mainstream fiction. Wim has a BFA in Theatre Arts and an MAT in English and Education from Drake University. Pat has a BA in English from Duke, an MA in Liberal Studies from Hollins University, and a PhD in Art Theory and Criticism from the University of Georgia. Both have classroom teaching experience. For 13 years they lived in the beautiful Mexican town of San Miguel de Allende, where they created and managed a scholarship program for at-risk students under the auspices of San Miguel PEN. Some of their stories draw on Mexican myth and tradition. Their highly-praised works for young readers include award-winning historical fiction, popular collections of plays, and a "nonfiction" book about unicorns.

*Away She Goes: Riding into Women's History*

**Publisher's Cataloging-In-Publication Data**
(Prepared by The Donohue Group, Inc.)

Coleman, Wim.
Away she goes : riding into women's history / by Wim Coleman and Pat Perrin ; illustrated by Valentina Belloni.

p. : ill. ; cm. -- (Setting the stage for fluency)

Summary: In the late 1800s, the bicycle first came to the United States from Europe. For women who either worked in factories or stayed at home, the bicycle liberated them like nothing ever has. This dramatization depicts how one two-wheeled invention changed fashion, opened doors, and led to a movement in women's rights still felt today. Includes special book features for further study and a special section for teachers and librarians.
Interest age level: 009-012.
Includes bibliographical references.
ISBN: 978-1-939656-56-8 (lib. binding/hardcover)
ISBN: 978-1-939656-58-2 (pbk.)
ISBN: 978-1-939656-57-5 (eBk)

1. Bicycles--Social aspects--United States--Juvenile drama. 2. Feminism--United States--History--Juvenile drama. 3. Bicycles and bicycling--Social aspects--United States--Drama. 4. Feminism--United States--History--Drama. 5. Children's plays, American. I. Perrin, Pat. II. Belloni, Valentina. III. Title.

PS3553.O47448 Aw 2014
[Fic]                                                        2013956251

This series first published by:
Red Chair Press LLC          PO Box 333          South Egremont, MA 01258-0333

Printed in the United States of America

1 2 3 4 5 18 17 16 15 14

# TABLE OF CONTENTS

# INTRODUCTION

In this play, a young girl named Kristy finds her great-great-great-grandmother's diary. As Kristy reads, the play unfolds, and she learns about life in earlier times.

In the 1900s, many people believed that women were naturally weak and timid. Both sports and too much thinking were considered unhealthy for them. So girls received less education than boys. Women did not have the right to vote in elections. And their clothing styles made activity difficult. They often wore tightly-laced corsets that made their waists look thinner. The bustle, a pad that made the back of the skirt bulge out, was still in style. Skirts were long and full. By the time of this story, that was all beginning to change.

One thing that led to change was the bicycle. A wooden bicycle was invented early in the 1800s. It was moved by the rider's feet on the ground. After that, bicycles took many shapes. Most had front and back wheels of different sizes.

The "safety bicycle" came along in the late 1800s. It had soft tires and was very much like our bicycles today. Women were attracted to the hugely popular new way to travel. But before women could ride bicycles, clothing styles had to change. Some beliefs had to change too.

# THE CAST OF CHARACTERS

**Kristy,** a girl in the present day, about 10 or 12 years old

**Molly,** Kristy's great-great-great-grandmother; between ages 12 and 42

**Bruce,** Molly's brother; between ages 15 and 46

**Mother,** Molly's Mother, Rose Betterton

**Father,** Molly's Father, Charles Betterton

**Libby,** Molly's aunt and Charles's sister, Libby Betterton

**Martin,** Molly's husband when she marries in 1919

**Susan B. Anthony,** a historical women's rights leader, 1820–1906

Setting: Port Jefferson, New York, and New York City

Time: Between 1894 and the present

## PROLOGUE

**Kristy:** What a discovery I made this summer! My mom and dad and I spent a couple of weeks in the old family home. It's in Port Jefferson, out on Long Island. One day I was looking through boxes in the storeroom. Can you guess what I found? An old leather-bound book. I opened it up and saw these hand-written words . . .

**Molly:** *(to diary)* Molly Betterton: Her Diary.

**Kristy:** Molly Betterton! That was my great-great-great-grandmother's maiden name! The most famous woman in our whole family! Here was my chance to find out about her life! I opened up the diary and looked at the first entry . . .

**Molly:** *(to diary)* August 18, 1890. My twelfth birthday.

**Kristy:** I kept right on reading, of course.

# SCENE ONE

**Molly:** *(to diary)* It's been a wonderful day, with a party and a cake. Mother made me a grown-up looking dress with big puffy sleeves. Father gave me a music box with a little ballerina that goes round and round. But my big brother, Bruce, gave me my favorite present: You! My new diary! I'll start by telling you something that happened yesterday. Oh, but don't tell anyone else, dear diary! Late in the afternoon, Bruce got home from his week at **boarding school**. He arrived on his bicycle. I met him at the **carriage house** as he was putting it away.

**Bruce:** So what do you want for your birthday, Little Sis?

**Molly:** Didn't you get me something already?

**Bruce:** Sure, but I want to make sure it's what you really want.

**Molly:** You know what I *really* want, Bruce. A ride on your bicycle.

**Bruce:** Oh, Molly, not that.

**Molly:** It doesn't look too hard.

**Bruce:** Well, maybe, but . . .

**Molly:** *(to diary)* It looked safe enough to me. The back wheel was only a little bigger than the front wheel. The seat was a good height for me. *(to Bruce)* So why can't I ride it?

**Bruce:** We'd both get in trouble.

**Molly:** But you do so many things that I can't do! You get to go away to school. I have to stay here and study with the **governess**.

**Bruce:** You get to learn French and play the piano. And paint with watercolors. And sew.

**Molly:** But I never leave the house! And the governess is so dull! Oh, please let me do this one little thing! And right now! Why not?

**Bruce:** Well, I guess you could sit on the handlebars while I . . .

**Molly:** I want to ride it all by myself.

**Bruce:** You know what Father says. Girls shouldn't do such things. It's unhealthy for them. And girls have no sense of balance.

**Molly:** Do you think that's true?

**Bruce:** He's a doctor. He ought to know.

**Molly:** *(to diary)* But I wouldn't give Bruce a moment's peace. I followed him all around the house. I kept begging and making myself a pest. Finally . . .

**Bruce:** All right, but let's not say anything to Father about this.

**Molly:** *(to diary)* We hurried back over to the carriage house. Bruce got his bicycle out again. He wheeled it over to the garden. I climbed up onto the seat, my long skirt hanging over each side. Bruce held the bicycle upright. He guided it along while I kept my feet on the pedals.

**Bruce:** Is this enough? Can we quit now?

**Molly:** Just let go of it.

**Bruce:** Oh, Sis, I can't do that.

**Molly:** I can balance it. I can feel it.

**Molly:** *(to diary)* Bruce didn't mean to let go. But I started pedaling, and the bicycle slipped out of his hands. And suddenly, I was riding on my own. I was pedaling through the garden.

**Bruce:** Well, look at that! Away she goes!

**Molly:** *(to diary)* And away I *did* go! Around and around the garden! I could handle the bicycle perfectly. But the frame was heavy. Riding was rough along the stone path. Suddenly my skirt got tangled up in the chain.

**Bruce:** Careful, Sis!

**Molly:** *(to diary)* The bicycle jumped to one side, and so did I. I steered away from a rosebush as I fell. I didn't want to get stuck all over with thorns. The bicycle fell over on top of me.

**Bruce:** Oh, look at you, Sis!

**Molly:** I'm all right.

**Bruce:** No, you're not! Your ankle is swelling up. Let's get you to the house.

# Scene Two

**Molly:** *(to diary)* Bruce helped me to my feet. I hung on his shoulder and limped along while he called out . . .

**Bruce:** Mother, come help!

**Molly:** *(to diary)* Mother stepped out onto the back porch.

**Mother:** Molly, what have you done now? Did you fall out of a tree again?

**Bruce:** It was the bicycle this time. It was my fault, Mother.

**Molly:** No, it wasn't!

**Bruce:** Do we need to take her to Father's office?

**Mother:** Maybe not. Let's get inside and see what we can do.

**Molly:** *(to diary)* Mother took us into the kitchen. She sat me down and put my foot high up on a chair. She opened the icebox and put some rags on the block of ice inside. When the rags got cold, she put them on my ankle.

**Mother:** It's not a bad sprain, thank goodness.

**Molly:** Soon Mother wrapped up my ankle in a bandage. She always knows just what to do at times like that. Back during the Civil War, she helped at an army hospital. She worked side by side with Father, who was a surgeon. And she wasn't much older than

I am now. While she was bandaging me up, I asked . . . *(to Mother)* Did you ever think about becoming a nurse, Mother?

**Mother:** If I had, I'd never have gotten married. How could I have kept a home, cooked meals, raised children? No, it was one thing or the other.

**Molly:** Was it a hard choice to make?

**Mother:** A little.

**Bruce:** Do we have to tell Father what happened?

**Mother:** Of course we do.

**Molly:** Oh, Mother . . .

**Mother:** We can't *lie* to him, anyway. Molly, stay off your feet and wear a skirt that covers the bandage. Maybe he won't notice.

**Molly:** *(to diary)* And he didn't notice. We were lucky.

# SCENE THREE

**Kristy:** I noticed that my grandmother's diary was marked by little ribbons. I opened it at one of the ribbons . . .

**Molly:** *(to diary)* August 18, 1894. My sixteenth birthday.

**Kristy:** Every ribbon marked a birthday. I kept reading . . .

**Molly:** *(to diary)* This has been no ordinary birthday, dear diary! The excitement started yesterday. Bruce and I were sitting on the front porch. He'd come home from college just for me. Wasn't that sweet of him?

**Bruce:** So what do you want for your birthday, Little Sis?

**Molly:** *(to diary)* Bruce always asks me that the day before my birthday. *(to Bruce)* Take me back to college with you.

**Bruce:** Oh, Sis, be serious.

**Molly:** Well, take me anywhere! New York, maybe. The city's so close, just sixty miles away, but we hardly ever go. And when we do go, I never get to do what I want. I could spend days and days

just roaming around Central Park. You don't know what it's like, staying in the house all day. I only get to learn things that will make me a proper wife. But you—you're going to be a lawyer!

**Bruce:** Maybe. That's still a long way off.

**Molly:** (*to diary*) Just then, a wagon pulled up, with some boxes in back. A woman was driving. She wore a very plain dress and hat. At first, I thought she was just some farm woman. But then she waved and called out . . .

**Libby:** Hallo there, Bruce. And Molly, is that you? Goodness, how you've grown!

**Molly:** (*to diary*) Bruce and I both recognized the freckles and the bright red hair.

**Bruce:** Aunt Libby!

**Molly:** You're here!

# SCENE FOUR

**Molly:** *(to diary)* Father came out onto the front porch.

**Charles:** Libby! Where on earth have you been?

**Libby:** You don't look happy to see me, Charlie.

**Molly:** *(to diary)* Bruce and I couldn't help but smile. Father *hated* it when she called him "Charlie."

**Father:** We were afraid you were dead.

**Molly:** *(to diary)* It's true, we were worried. About a year and a half ago, Libby's husband died. He left her a pretty large fortune. Then suddenly Libby disappeared. Nobody knew what happened to her. Until now, anyway. She climbed down off the wagon and hugged each of us.

**Libby:** It's so good to see you!

**Charles:** Why don't you have a man to drive that carriage?

**Libby:** It just didn't occur to me, I guess. I've been traveling every which way for the last year or so. Ships, trains, balloons. Horseback, camel-back, and elephant-back too. And rickshaws. Have you ever heard of rickshaws—little carts pulled by men? I rode those in India and China and Japan. And motorcars. Have you ever ridden a motorcar?

**Molly:** Have you?

**Libby:** I've driven one! So much power and speed! I must have gone 10 or 12 miles an hour!

# SCENE FIVE

**Molly:** *(to diary)* Mother served everyone iced tea on the porch. We sat and listened to Aunt Libby. Why, she'd traveled all the way around the world! And all by herself! She told us about the great cities of Europe. And the Sahara Desert in Africa. And the beautiful temples of India. And the Great Wall of China. And the islands of the Pacific. I was excited—and maybe a little jealous too. But Father didn't like what he heard.

**Father:** You'll never change, Libby. You get an itch to do something, and away you go! We'd had such hopes when you got married. We thought you'd become a proper lady. But no. And I suppose you still think women should have the right to vote.

**Libby:** I certainly do, Charlie.

**Father:** If only Alexander hadn't died so young.

**Libby:** Yes, it is a pity, isn't it? He could have tagged along with me around the world.

**Father:** But what are these boxes you've brought along?

**Libby:** You'll see in good time. Tomorrow's your birthday, isn't it, Molly? So I have time to make you your birthday present. Rose, you've still got a sewing machine, haven't you?

**Mother:** Of course.

**Libby:** Let me get my fabrics together, and I'll get started.

**Molly:** *(to diary)* Bruce helped Libby get some fabrics off the wagon. She went into the house with them. Soon we heard the sewing machine clanking away in the storeroom.

**Father:** Sewing? Libby? She's never done such a thing!

**Molly:** *(to diary)* Mother laughed . . .

**Mother:** Maybe Libby is turning out to be a proper lady after all, Charles.

**Molly:** *(to diary)* Aunt Libby kept on sewing. She stopped only long enough to have dinner with the rest of us.

**Kristy:** I kept reading about Molly's sixteenth birthday . . .

**Molly:** *(to diary)* Aunt Libby didn't go to bed until late that night. At dawn she got up and started sewing again. She took a break to eat breakfast, then went right back to work. After breakfast, I tried on the new dress that Mother had made for me.

**Mother:** How do you like it?

**Molly:** It's lovely, Mother. Thank you so much.

**Mother:** I wanted it to be special.

**Molly:** *(to diary)* It was the most grown-up dress I'd ever worn. It looked beautiful in the full-length mirror. But I'm afraid Mother noticed how uncomfortable I felt.

**Mother:** It takes some getting used to, doesn't it?

**Molly:** The corset's so tight . . .

**Mother:** Yes, it's a bit hard to breathe.

**Molly:** . . . and the bustle's so big . . .

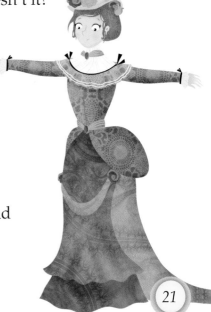

**Mother:** I know. It makes you feel bulky. But it makes your waist look tiny.

**Molly:** . . . and the train drags along behind me. I'm afraid to walk around. I might break something.

**Mother:** You'll be fine. Remember, it's all part of being a proper young lady.

**Molly:** *(to diary)* Before my party, I peeked into the storeroom. Libby was still sewing away. *(to Libby)* Aren't you joining us for the party, Aunt Libby?

**Libby:** Oh, goodness, is it time already? I'm afraid I'm not finished yet. Hang on, I'll be there as soon as I can.

**Molly:** *(to diary)* The parlor was filled with guests, all dressed in their finest clothes. Mother had invited all of Port Jefferson's suitable young men. After all, I'm sixteen years old. It's time to start looking for a husband. A pianist began to play, and the guests cleared the floor. One by one, the gentlemen asked me to dance. I'm afraid it didn't go very well. I'd grown so tall during the last couple of years. I towered over most of them. And—oh, dear diary, don't tell anybody else this, please! The young men of Port Jefferson are all so boring!

**Bruce:** Where's Aunt Libby?

**Mother:** Still sewing, I believe.

**Molly:** *(to diary)* Aunt Libby kept sewing in the storeroom all through the party. She came out when the last guests were leaving. She had a new outfit folded up and ready for me. We went to my room, and I tried it on.

**Libby:** Do you like it?

**Molly:** Well, it's . . . very comfortable. Thank you so much. Is it to sleep in?

**Libby:** No, silly! It's for outdoors!

**Molly:** *(to diary)* I'd never worn or seen such an outfit. The blouse and jacket were comfortable. And they didn't look too odd. But instead of a skirt, I had on loose-fitting trousers. They fastened just below my knees. *(to Libby)* What kind of pants are these?

**Libby:** It's a new fashion. Bloomers, they're sometimes called. But they're also called "rationals." Because what rational woman wouldn't want to wear them? Don't you feel much better than you did a few minutes ago?

**Molly:** *(to diary)* It was true. I was so tired of that heavy bustle and train following me around all day. And it was so easy to breathe without that awful corset. The whole outfit felt free and comfortable.

**Libby:** Come on. Let's show it to your family.

**Molly:** *(to diary)* We went to the parlor, where Mother, Father, and Bruce were waiting. Mother and Bruce smiled.

**Mother:** Oh, Libby, you've made her "rationals"! How charming!

**Bruce:** You look grand, Little Sis!

**Molly:** *(to diary)* But Father was shocked.

**Father:** Thank goodness the guests are gone! I certainly hope she's not leaving the house in that outfit.

**Libby:** Why not?

**Father:** It's shocking!

**Libby:** How so?

**Mother:** Isn't she covered up decently?

**Father:** Well, yes.

**Mother:** So what's the problem?

**Molly:** *(to diary)* Poor Father didn't know what to say. I thanked Aunt Libby again.

**Libby:** Oh, but there's another present to go with it. You'll get it tomorrow morning.

## SCENE EIGHT

**Kristy:** I turned the page to see what happened the next day . . .

**Molly:** *(to diary)* I've never had a day like this, dear diary! As soon as I got out of bed, I put on my new outfit. I joined the family for breakfast. But I noticed something odd . . . *(to family)* Where is Aunt Libby?

**Mother:** She had breakfast before the rest of us. She said she'd meet you at the carriage house when you finished eating.

**Molly:** *(to diary)* I ate breakfast quickly. Then Bruce, Mother, Father, and I went out to the carriage house. Aunt Libby was there, dressed in "rationals" just like mine. And she was holding a bicycle. It looked different from Bruce's bicycle. The front and back wheels were the same size.

**Libby:** Here it is—your other gift.

**Molly:** Oh, Aunt Libby, it's grand, but . . .

**Libby:** What's the matter?

**Bruce:** I'm afraid Molly had a bad experience on my bicycle.

**Libby:** Oh, Bruce, your old thing. That was never meant for girls. Or for women, for that matter. This bicycle is new and different. It's even called a "safety bicycle." See for yourself, Molly.

**Molly:** *(to diary)* She rolled the bicycle to me, and I took hold of it. What a surprise! *(to Libby)* Why, it's not heavy at all! I could lift it with just one hand!

**Libby:** It's made of lightweight metal. And look at the wheels.

**Molly:** They're not iron, like on Bruce's bicycle. They're made of rubber.

**Libby:** Rubber with air inside. It's smooth to ride on. And you're perfectly dressed for it. Try it!

**Molly:** *(to diary)* Before I knew it, I was riding the bicycle around and around the garden. There wasn't any danger of my "rationals" getting caught in the chain.  It was so fun and easy, I laughed out loud. When I stopped to catch my breath, I saw that Aunt Libby was sitting on a bicycle of her own.

**Libby:** So where do you want to go, Molly?

**Molly:** *(to diary)* My mind reeled! Where *couldn't* we go on these marvelous things? *(to Libby)* I—I don't know, Aunt Libby.

**Bruce:** I know where she wants to go. To New York. To Central Park.

**Father:** Good heavens, son! Have you lost your mind? Have you *all* lost your minds?

**Libby:** It sounds reasonable to me. We can take a couple of days getting there. I know where we can spend the night.

**Father:** Bicycles are bad for women's health.

**Libby:** Have you treated a lot of women for bicycle health problems, Charlie?

**Father:** No.

**Libby:** Do you know any doctors who ever did?

**Father:** No, but—

**Libby:** So how do you know this, Charlie?

**Father:** Well, it's—it's common sense. Women are so **fragile**.

**Libby:** I've ridden horses, donkeys, elephants, camels—and bicycles. I've been all around the world. Do I look any the less healthy for it?

**Father:** But the two of you, traveling alone . . .

**Mother:** How fast can these bicycles go, Libby?

**Libby:** When they really get going? Even faster than a motorcar.

**Mother:** Then let them go, Charles. They'll be safe as long as they're on their bicycles. Libby knows how to look after the both of them.

**Molly:** *(to diary)* Father couldn't say anything else against it. Soon Libby and I had packed up just enough things for a couple of days on the road. And I brought you along, dear diary! As we rode away from the house, I heard Bruce shout out . . .

**Bruce:** Away she goes!

**Molly:** *(to diary)* We rode all day today. We just now stopped in Huntington at a nice little inn. We'll stay the night here. Tomorrow we'll be in New York City. Miles and miles of beautiful paths await us in Central Park. I've never felt so free!

## SCENE NINE

**Kristy:** I already knew quite a lot about the rest of Grandmother Molly's life. She grew up to be a famous journalist and author. She married Martin, a magazine publisher. They lived happily in New York City and had a daughter, Elise. Elise was my great-great grandmother. I skipped ahead in Molly's diary to a ribbon marking another birthday . . .

**Molly:** *(to diary)* August 18, 1920. I turn forty-two today. And such an amazing birthday! I believe it's my best birthday since . . . Well, since when, dear diary? Since Aunt Libby bought me that bicycle when I was sixteen, I believe. Martin threw a party for me this evening. Elise is away for her first year at Elmira Female College, so she wasn't here. I didn't expect a surprise in the morning. Martin had already gone to the office. I was sitting in the den typing a story. The phone rang. *(to telephone)* Hello?

**Bruce:** Hello, Little Sis! Happy Birthday!

**Molly:** Thank you, Big Brother.

**Bruce:** I see that the whole country gave you a great present today.

**Molly:** What do you mean?

**Bruce:** Haven't you seen the newspaper?

**Molly:** I haven't opened it yet.

**Bruce:** Then look. I'll stay on the phone.

**Molly:** *(to diary)* I opened up the newspaper and . . .
*(to telephone)* Oh, my goodness! The Nineteenth Amendment to the Constitution! It's been **ratified** by all the states! It's a law at last!

**Bruce:** That's right, Sis. Now you have the right to vote! So do all American women! How do you like your birthday present?

**Molly:** *(to diary)* I choked up and couldn't talk for a few seconds. Tears came to my eyes. I thought about Aunt Libby. Like me and so many other women, she'd fought hard for this amendment. How I wished she were alive to see this day.

**Bruce:** Are you still there, Molly?

**Molly:** Yes. This is wonderful.

**Bruce:** Let's both take a holiday. I'll meet you at Central Park in a half hour.

**Molly:** Where in the park?

**Bruce:** Why, Girls' Gate, of course!

**Molly:** *(laughing)* How perfect!

**Molly:** *(to diary)* I left the apartment on my bicycle. I made my way among the motorcars to Central Park. It only took a few minutes to get there. Bruce was already at Girls' Gate. And right beside him on his own bicycle was . . . *(to Martin)* Martin, dear! You're here too!

**Martin:** Do you think I'd stay at work on your very special day, darling?

**Molly:** The three of us rode our bikes through the beautiful park. My husband and brother and I talked as we rode.

**Martin:** You and this new amendment are actually the same age, aren't you, Molly?

**Molly:** How do you figure that?

**Martin:** It was written by Elizabeth Cady Stanton and Susan B. Anthony in 1878.

**Bruce:** The year you were born!

**Martin:** And now their dream has come true!

**Molly:** *(to diary)* I thought about Susan B. Anthony as we rode along. I remembered something she said about women and bicycles back in 1896 . . .

**Voice of Susan B. Anthony:** I think the bicycle has done more to **emancipate** women than anything else in the world. It gives a woman a feeling of freedom and **self-reliance**. . . . Away she goes, the picture of free, **untrammeled** womanhood.

**Molly:** *(to diary)* I also remembered when I was twelve. The first time I rode Bruce's bike. How I pulled away from him and went riding on my own. But today was different. Now I wouldn't fall. I started pedaling faster. I couldn't seem to help it. I heard Bruce call out behind me . . .

**Bruce:** Away she goes!

**Kristy:** And there's so much more to read in Grandmother Molly's diary! And so much history in it too!

# WORDS TO KNOW

**boarding school:** a school where students live while taking classes

**carriage house:** a building for keeping horse-drawn carriages

**emancipate:** set free, in this case from social rules

**fragile:** easily broken

**governess:** a woman hired to teach children at home

**prologue:** an introduction to a play or book

**ratified:** made officially valid.

**self-reliance:** depending on oneself, not on others

**untrammeled:** not held back

## Learn More about Women's History

**Books:**

Macy, Sue. Wheels of Change: *How Women Rode the Bicycle to Freedom.* National Geographic, 2011.

Zheutlin, Peter. *Around the World on Two Wheels: Annie Londonderry's Extraordinary Ride.* Citadel Press, 2008.

**Web Sites:**

**The Wheelmen, for the enjoyment and preservation of our bicycling heritage:** the wheelmen.org.

**Women on Wheels:** http://www.annielondonderry.com/womenWheels.

**Places**

**Bicycle Museum of America,** New Bremen, Ohio.

The National **Women's History Museum,** Washington, DC

**The Susan B. Anthony House,** national landmark home and headquarters, Rochester, New York.